A Powerful **5 Step Money Plan** to Financial Health and Wealth Now

# YOUNG MONEY PLANNER

## Helping You Build a
## Better Financial Future Now

# TODD ROMER

# YOUNG MONEY PLANNER:
## A POWERFUL 5 STEP MONEY PLAN
## TO FINANCIAL HEALTH AND WEALTH NOW

Helping You Build a Better Financial Future Now

by Todd Romer

ISBN 978-0-9906865-0-7

The Young Money Planner is a personal guidebook that compliments the Young Money book. The Planner is meant to help you take the necessary action steps to create real financial health and to start achieving financial wealth over the long term.

net worlding
PUBLISHING

www.networlding.com

# DEDICATION

This planner is dedicated to my wife Jaci and my four kids Jack, Luke, Alec and Mia. All of you have provided unwavering support of my dream of helping young people master money at an early age so they can focus more on their life's real purpose and dream like never before.

# TABLE OF CONTENTS

## YOUNG MONEY

# A Powerful 5 Step Money Plan to Financial Health and Wealth Now

*This planner is based on the Young Money book. The book, along with this planner, provides a distinct money management system for young adults to follow to achieve financial health, create wealth over time, and find purpose in their life.*

## The Problem

Chances are you're one of the millions of high school or college students that aren't getting one of the most important tools you'll need to succeed in life, or business—money management.

Currently only a fraction of high schools and colleges teach personal finance to their students. As a result the 42 million 17-29 year old young adults in the US have received little knowledge. capability, confidence or comfort when it comes to money management and personal finance. If you're not worried about money, or think you've got a handle on what to do with it, consider this research:

- 1,000 first-year college students scored an average of 65 or a D on a traditional grading scale on the Inceptia National Financial Aptitude Analysis in 2012.
- 85% percent of college grads plan to move back home after graduating. (Twentysomething Inc. 2010 survey) The rate has risen from sixty-seven percent in 2006. (Jessica Dickler, CNN staff writer).
- 93% percent of American parents with teenagers report worrying that their children might make financial missteps such as overspending or living beyond their means. (Charles Schwab's "Parents & Money" survey.)
- 86% of students would rather learn about money before making real world mistakes. (Charles Schwab Survey).

How did this happen? In the last fifteen years corporations, nonprofits and government entities have spent hundreds of millions of dollars teaching financial literacy. But they're seeing little, if any, change in financial knowledge and aptitude. Our research has discovered the following problems that include:

- The training has not been the right training—it is not training supported with specific financial behavioral change action steps.
- I mean no disrespect to those conducting training now, but the training is boring!
- The training hasn't focused on what matters— the core component of an effective program.

But there is good news! Young adults do have the desire to become more financially healthy and to learn how to create wealth over time. In fact, according to YPulse Lifeline (2013) 97% of Millennials (ages 17-29) want to plan more for their future.

Research has shown that as student loan debt increases to all-time highs, Millennials will have more interest in personal finance (MediaPost Communications 2013). Even better, how to save for retirement, basic investing, and how loans work were the top three topics Millennials wish they had learned more about in school (Forbes 2013).

A recent survey of 65,000 college students shows the need and interest to have financial education administered early on in the college experience to maximize the likelihood that students will make sound financial decisions and increase their chance of degree completion. (Money Matters On Campus Survey (2014) Administered By EverFi and Sponsored by Higher One)

# The Five Steps

In the Young Money Planner, you will be presented with five steps. Each of the steps correlates with a chapter from the book. You may use the book as a guide as you work your way through the planner. The five steps are listed below:

Chapter 1: Step One – Make a Decision to Dream
Chapter 2: Step Two – Automatic Savings Leads to Financial Health
Chapter 3: Step Three – Just Say No Sometimes
Chapter 4: Step Four – Get into the Game of Investing Automatically
Chapter 5: Step Five – Pay Yourself Second
Chapter 6: Other Personal Financial Stuff
Chapter 7: More Personal Financial Stuff
Chapter 8: Entrepreneur Mindset – A Must Have to Get Ahead with Money
Chapter 9: The Young Money Plan Movement and 5 Point Checklist

# CHAPTER 1: STEP ONE
# Make a Decision to Dream

## Introduction

This is the mother of all steps and key to creating financial health and wealth. Financial well-being begins with knowing your WHY. Why do you want to be financially successful? Your WHY is tied to your dreaming. I want to encourage you to start dreaming, small at first, then BIG! This builds financial confidence no matter how young or old you are. You'll find out how to create concrete, realistic financial and even life goals. These short-term and long-term financial goals or dreams will serve as your motivation for creating and maintaining financial health and building wealth over time.

One of the main issues that many young people have is fear. Yes, even in this era of having access to all kinds of knowledge, many young people are scared of investing their money. As we read in the book, many young people hear stories of how people lost money investing in various things, such as stocks, real estate, or a new business. Do these statements sound familiar? If the answer is yes, today is the day to change that mindset. You have a lot of goals. This is your WHY for making different financial choices.

## Short-Term Financial Goals

In our culture today we hear messages like "dream big baby dream big." I fully encourage you to dream big. However, many people who have dreamed big only in their minds and did not establish short term goals or "small dreams" first ended up backing down on their big dreams because the road early on got a little rough . Their confidence in themselves took a hit and they made a choice to retreat from their dream.

By setting small short-term financial goals, first, you will build your confidence to then set bigger, long-term financial goals. We are all creatures of habit. Our habits are developed through our actions. At first you may not feel happy about sacrificing through saving, even if it is only small amounts of money. But, as you save a little at a time for a short-term financial goal of say $250 in one month, once you achieve this goal, you will very likely have a feeling of satisfaction and some initial but important confidence.

## EXERCISE #1

Let's get started on determining your WHYs. Many times people fear they do not make enough money to even think about saving, but you may be surprised at how much you can save despite your income. Brainstorm five financial goals that you would like to accomplish within the next year regardless of your income. I have provided examples in the left column.

| Short-Term Goals (Less than one year) | Short-Term Goals (Less than one year) |
|---|---|
| Goal #1<br>Open a checking account & set-up automatic savings (see Chapter 2) | Goal #1 |
| Goal #2<br>Open a savings account | Goal #2 |
| Goal #3<br>Save 5% of my income each paycheck | Goal #3 |
| Goal #4<br>Start a 401K (if employed) | Goal #4 |
| Goal #5<br>Start a car savings account | Goal #5 |

# Mid-Range Financial Goals

Now you can move on to your next set of goals—what I call your Mid-Range Goals. These goals lay the foundation for you to continue believing in yourself and getting closer to know your personal WHY in life.

This is where you should again connect with your "WHY" and apply it to your Young Money Plan. The energy to stay committed will come from recommitting to your purpose or WHY. It's easy to lose sight of your goals. How do you carry your dreams and put them front and center in your life on a daily basis? Life is distracting and knowing how to keep your dreams in front of you often is empowering.

## EXERCISE #2

Exercise #2 is important because you really start to connect the WHY and begin to apply it here in the plan. One of the reasons why your mid-range goals are so important is because you need to find the commitment to see these goals through. The timeframe is longer and likely the amount you need to save will also be larger. Exercise #2 will have several different steps. Let's get started!

In the table below, list your Top Three mid-range goals.

| Mid-Range Goals (1 to 5 years) | Mid-Range Goals (1 to 5 years) |
|---|---|
| Goal #1<br><br>*Save $5,000 within 1 year to put towards a new or used car* | Goal #1 |
| Goal #2<br><br>*Save $5,000-$10,000 in the next 3 years for a new apartment or new furniture* | Goal #2 |
| Goal #3<br><br>*Save $25,000-$35,000 in 5 years for a down payment for a first home.* | Goal #3 |

Now that you have decided your mid-range goals, you can now consider how much money you need to save and how you will save this money. Complete the following table to organize your finances in relation to the goals.

| Mid-Range Goals (1 to 5 years) & Money Required | Action Plan to Save the Money |
|---|---|
| Goal #1 | |
| Goal #2 | |
| Goal #3 | |

# EXERCISE #3

Learning to save money is a lifetime event. One way to accomplish this goal of learning to save money is to journal your progress. Write in your journal daily. In fact, write in it the first thing every morning, even if it is only for one minute. Write down the amount you have saved. For example, "I have already saved $200 and I am working toward now saving $500. I am grateful that I continue to save and I am committed to reaching all of my goals."

For this exercise use the journal pages at the back of this planner. The important point is to write in your journal daily to ensure that you stay on-target. Here are some additional steps that you can take.

- **Look in the mirror daily and state your commitment.** It may sound really funny but looking into your own eyes and making a commitment to yourself will have a powerful effect on you. It will touch your heart, the location where your commitment will be the most strongly felt. Then whenever you stray from your commitment, for example, getting that extra clothing purchase you didn't need right now, you can connect back to this moment in the mirror and regain your confidence.
- **Get a mentor or coach.** Think about who you know. Is there someone you look up to? If so, ask them to mentor or coach you in this area of your life. If not, find someone through other friends or family. Meet as often as you feel is necessary, maybe weekly at first and then monthly as you gain confidence.
- **Join Young Money University.** This online community will be full of people just like you who have a desire to get ahead financially and reach their goals and dreams. A great place to be real, receive encouragement and have access to tools and resources to get you where you want to go.
- **If you fall, get back up!** If you are like me, you are going to make mistakes. Don't wait. Get help as soon as you see your commitment is sliding. Spent too much? Call your mentor for an emergency meeting to get back on track.

For the entire process, having a mentor can help you immensely. I would suggest finding a mentor as soon as possible. Make sure to share the Planner with your mentor. At the end of the Planner, there will be a place for you to report your progress and also for your mentor to report your progress.

# Long-Term Financial Goals

It is time to think about the long-term landscape. So what happens next? What does the ultimate path of a successful young person look like?

## EXERCISE #4

For Exercise #4, you will list some of your long term financial goals which could be 10, 15 or 25 years out.

| Long-Term Goals | Long-Term Goals |
|---|---|
| Goal #1<br>*Start my own business - $35,000 - $75,000 (10 years)* | Goal #1 |
| Goal #2<br>*My wedding - $10,000 - $20,000 (5 - 10 years)* | Goal #2 |
| Goal #3<br>*Pay off home mortgage early - $100,000 - $150,000 (15 years)* | Goal #3 |
| Goal #4<br>*College fund for my kids - $75,000 - $125,000 (25 years)* | Goal #4 |
| Goal #5<br>*Early retirement - $750,000 - $1.5 million (25 -30 years)* | Goal #5 |

Now that you have decided your long-term financial goals, you can now consider how much money you need to save and how you will save this money. Complete the following table to organize your finances in relation to the goals.

| Long-Term Goals & Money Required | Action Plan to Save the Money |
| --- | --- |
| Goal #1 | |
| Goal #2 | |
| Goal #3 | |
| Goal #4 | |
| Goal #5 | |

## Get Dreaming

Now that you have gone through Step One, what will you do? If you care about yourself enough I believe you will "get dreaming." In other words, you will take what you know now, which should be different from what you knew when you started reading this chapter, and move forward.

One step at a time, which is how the next chapters are laid out, move forward with me. Learn what thousands of other young adults like yourself have learned ... that it's better to start now than to wait.

*The future belongs to those who believe in the beauty of their dreams.* **— Eleanor Roosevelt**

## Additional Action Step

Make A Decision To Dream. Fill out your own online "dream sheet" by going to **www.youngmoneyplan.com**. List both your small and big dreams/goals. Set specific financial goals (i.e....I want to own a breakfast cafe by age 30 (Big Dream/Goal) or I want to save $2,500 as a down payment on a new/used car within 12 months (Small Dream/Goal).

Once you have filled this out, print out a copy and put it up on where you can see it daily—your mirror in your bathroom, your refrigerator or even both.

## What's Next?

I've shared with you the importance of connecting to your purpose—your WHY. I've also shared the landscape of the overall savings plan that works. What's next? Now that you are beginning to discover your dreams and aspirations, both for your finances and your life, it's time to start saving. In Chapter 2 and Step Two, I'll help you learn why automatic saving is super important and how to get started.

# CHAPTER 2: STEP TWO

# Automatic Savings Leads to Financial Health

In Step Two, you will see how an automatic savings plan can lead you more rapidly than any other thing you can do to financial health. For many young people with whom I've worked, this is instrumental to their success. We will explore why this works and how you can best achieve success with this simple strategy.

It's been said so often that it feels like a cliché, but that does not make it any less true: We live in a society that values and even demands instant gratification. In so many ways we are told from a very young age that we can demand and even get anything we want immediately. Unfortunately, instant gratification often gives us pleasure in the short term but does not provide true satisfaction or happiness in the long term.

In some ways this desire for instant gratification and happiness through purchasing is not your fault. Most Americans have been acculturated from a young age to think 'buy, buy, buy' is the way to contentment. So many forces in our culture have conditioned us to buy into the dual lie: that material goods will somehow lead to happiness and that we deserve to have whatever we want immediately. But you are an adult now, and you can choose to opt out of this lie.

Although our brains might tell us it is all a lie, for many of us our hearts still equate spending money with success and happiness. This is true for many, many people in our society, but it's especially true for young adults who do not have the tools or experience to see through the lies. When we would be better off saving and even investing, we are spending on things that we certainly do not need in the pursuit of a kind of happiness that can never be attained by spending anyway.

So what can you do? The emotion can be so overpowering that even when people know they should save, rather than spend, they often spend anyway. How can you be a wise manager of money and bypass the emotion? In a nutshell, how can you become a saver rather than a spender?

# Automatic Savings: A Way to Battle Natural Temptation

With all the emotional associations that many Americans have with money it makes it incredibly easy to spend any income that they have. It is almost as though as soon as the money comes into their hands, it slips out through their fingers. Even if people want to save, the temptation to spend is nearly overpowering. The emotions we have tied up with acquiring and spending money are incredibly powerful and addictive even. So what can you do?

The answer lies in automatic savings. Sometimes this is presented as the advice to "pay yourself first." Here's the deal: when you receive a paycheck, the entire amount should not go into a checking account to be spent during the next two weeks or month, before your next paycheck. Instead, you must immediately set aside part of each paycheck in a savings account. Then, do not touch the money in your savings account. In some ways, you want to behave as though the money in this savings account does not exist; certainly you want to behave as though dipping into it and spending it is simply a non-negotiable.

## EXERCISE #1

As we have discussed, it is important to have automatic savings each pay period. One or the reasons this is so important because if you have the option and have to transfer the money yourself, it is likely you won't do it. Yes, that sounds harsh, but you will think about the other places the money could go and not deposit the money into your savings account. Automatic savings takes you out of the equation. When you receive your direct deposit for your paycheck, the savings automatically goes to your savings account and the rest to your checking account. For Exercise #1, you will consider how much money you can start saving with your next paycheck. One way to create money to save is to cut back on your spending. To get started, answer the following questions:

For this activity, you will have the opportunity to consider ways that you can cut back and save money. Complete the following questions.

1. Brainstorm and think of the top 5 things that you purchase daily, a couple times a week, or weekly that you could live without.

   a. _____

   b. _____

   c. _____

   d. _____

   e. _____

2. For each of the five items that you identified, calculate how much money you would save weekly if you cut back on those items.

   a. _____

   b. _____

   c. _____

d. _____

e. _____

**3.** Of the five items that you identified, which item will you start with and why have you chosen that item? _____

_____

_____

After completing this activity, you should now have an amount that you can save each week. Before your next paycheck, request to have this amount automatically direct deposited in your savings account. Or just as easy have this amount automatically transferred from your checking to your savings account each month. See how easy that was!

# Your "Money Engine"

You must open up a checking and savings account if you want to follow the Young Money Plan for yourself. Neither account should cost you anything. Let's face it a checking account is not very exciting. In fact for some of you who have a checking account already it represents some pain because we primarily use our checking account to pay bills. But I want you to think differently about your checking account going forward.

Your checking account should now be viewed as your "money engine," the piece that is moving you forward, day to day. There are two important pieces of this analogy. An engine keeps things going, and an engine is non-personal and emotionless. Treating your checking account as an engine allows you to save and spend wisely. It also helps you remove the troubling emotions that are too often associated with money.

We will talk more about budgeting later, but you should know right now that the source of your monthly budget is this checking account. You will use your checking account to pay for day-to-day expenses and regular bills. In this way, your checking account continues to function like an engine, allowing you to chug forward each day.

Most employers offer, and some even require, direct deposit of paychecks for their employees. If you are not currently using direct deposit for your paycheck, I strongly recommend that you do so right away. This saves you the hassle of having to make a trip to the bank to deposit a check, but it also allows you to set up a system where a portion of your check is automatically transferred to your savings account.

For many of you that are not working a steady job because you are a full time student but you still have some monthly income you can tell your bank or credit union to begin automatically transferring money from your checking to your savings account every month. You can choose the date such as the 15th or 25th of each month. It is simple to set up by walking into your branch, calling them or doing it online.

This point may be the most important point of this entire Step Two: open a checking and savings account and then have a percentage of your monthly income (I recommend at least 10%) automatically transferred to this savings account. No matter how small your paychecks may be, you must routinely set aside a portion of each paycheck into a savings account OR have an automatic monthly transfer take place from your checking to your savings account which is now what I like to call a "life happens" account.

## EXERCISE #2

As we discussed in the book, it is important to have a savings account. This means that you have enough money for six months to pay all of your bills. For this activity, think about your savings account and answer the following questions:

1. Do you have a savings account? _____

2. If yes, how long have you had the account and what is the average balance? _____
   _____

3. If no, what has stopped you from opening an account? _____
   _____

4. If you have not opened up a savings account, record here when you have. This only takes a few minutes, so go online to your bank or credit union or visit your local branch. Come back to this page and record when you have your savings account.

   _____

   _____

There are many online, national, regional or local banks that can get you set up on Step 2 to create an automatic savings plan for you. A few that I like include:

### CAPITAL ONE 360
capitalone360.com

Both the savings and checking account have no fees or minimums. With your checking account you receive a debit card, you can make mobile deposits and you have access to over 36,000 fee free ATM"s and 2,000 Capital One ATM"s. You can have multiple savings accounts and create a nickname for each of them. This enables you to automatically save per month into multiple named savings accounts which will really keep you on track financially. When you put a name such as "Travel", "New Phone" or "Future Car" to virtually every dollar the chances of you taking money out of your "Travel" savings account to spend on new shoes or dinner out again with your friends will be pretty low.

### PNC BANK – VIRTUAL WALLET
pnc.com/virtual-wallet

Virtual Wallet from PNC Bank provides you with three accounts. Your Spend account is your checking account which comes with a debit card and access to over 7,200 ATM's to withdraw money with no fee Your Reserve account is for short term savings and your Growth account is for long term savings for larger purchases down the road. There is a $7.00 per month fee but that is waived if you maintain an average monthly balance of $500 or if you have at least $500 of monthly direct deposit to your Spend account.

## BBVA COMPASS – CLEAR CONNECT
bbvacompass.com

Having a large regional presence, BBVA Compass bank stays ahead of the curve by offering a very simple, all digital and mobile savings and checking account platform with Clear Connect. A minimum of $25 deposit to open up a savings or checking account but no monthly fees as long as you bank primarily online or through your smartphone.

## FIFTH THIRD BANK – GOAL SETTER SAVINGS
53.com

With a Goal Setter Savings account you set a personal savings goal, save at your own pace and track your progress online. When you reach your goal you get an interest bonus. These days any kind of bonus is sweet. The eAccess checking account is ideal if you primarily do all of your banking online and rarely write a check, which is very common of young people today. eAccess checking comes with a free debit card, free mobile banking and text alerts (ie....you get a text if your balance is below a predetermined amount) and access to over 2,400 free Fifth Third ATM's.

## ALLY BANK
ally.com

Another online bank that offers mobile savings and checking accounts with above average interest rates. Not that today's interest rates on savings or checking will make you rich soon. Ally Bank has mobile check deposit, no minimum deposit required and no monthly maintenance fees. You can also can send people money using their Person to Person payment platform called PopMoney by only needing someone's mobile phone number or email address.

## CREDIT UNIONS

Your local credit union can also help you with Step 2 and setting up automatic savings. Many young people are not aware that credit unions are a financial institution just like a bank. Credit unions have been around for several decades and their numbers keep growing. The major differences between a bank and a credit union is that when you join a credit union you become a member/owner and credit unions are designated non-profit organizations. Credit unions also see themselves as different from mainstream banks with a mission to be community oriented, to serve people and not focused solely on profit.

   Over the last 10 years credit unions have been doing a good job of offering younger consumers relevant banking products and services including online and mobile banking, bill pay and person to person payments. Recently credit unions have created a shared network of branches and ATM's that allow members to do their banking in nearly all 50 states with little to no fees.

# Action Steps

In addition to the exercises above, complete the following action steps in order to successfully complete Step Two.

- Recognize the various ways that emotions are connected to how you approach money. Realize that many of these emotions come from lies that the culture has fed you whether you're conscious of them or not!
- Set up separate checking and savings accounts, either at a traditional bank, an online bank, or a credit union.
- Once your accounts are set up, create an automatic transfer from checking to savings each month. Whether through direct deposit from your employer or you set up directly with your bank or credit union.
- Base your monthly budget on what is in your checking account only. Do not even think of using savings for monthly expenses. Your savings account is your "life happens" account, to be used for emergencies and unplanned expenses only!

# What's Next?

Now that you have set up separate checking and savings accounts and have money automatically going towards savings, what do you do next to create financial security?

Step Three of the Young Money Planner includes thoughtful spending and the practice of setting up and sticking to a budget. It is really a matter of self-control and saying, "No Sometimes." And it's not always easy, but it certainly pays off.

# CHAPTER 3: STEP THREE
# Just Say No Sometimes

Money can be very emotional for many people. I'll show you how to let go of emotions that hinder your financial wellness and success and how to become more money aware.

I'll also show you how to create a realistic spending plan or budget, one that you can live with and that does not stifle your daily life.

Now that you have your accounts set-up after completing Step Two, your next step is to set up a monthly budget. This budget allows you to clearly understand where you are spending your money. It also allows you to say no to things that you may want but certainly don't need.

## Needs Vs. Wants

Let's begin by thinking about the difference between needs and wants. This distinction is important because many people run into money difficulty by not distinguishing between the two.

Now, of course, you know the difference: a need is something that is essential to your survival, something that humans require in order to live in a healthy fashion, while a want is something that you can live equally as well without. It's really that simple. The problem is that many people do not stop and think about this difference before making a purchase. And the truth is that our needs, as opposed to wants, make up a pretty short list: food, basic clothing, a place to live, health care. Of course, humans have other needs—love, friendship—that money truly cannot buy.

Additionally, you should consider that while you have legitimate needs--food, clothing, shelter--you can generally choose to meet these needs in ways that make either more or less economic sense. Now, am I saying that you are only allowed to spend money on needs and not spend anything on wants? Of course not. But realizing what you truly need, is a first step towards saying no to things that you don't need. It's also a way to begin to think about budgeting, for a budget is really just a way of prioritizing where and how we spend money, realizing that we pay for needs before wants.

## EXERCISE #1

Here's a list of items. Decide whether they are wants or needs. Some things to think about as you make your choices – Do you really need it? Can you live without it? Few incomes are big enough to cover all of your wants, so choices must be made. Please a "x" in the appropriate box.

| Need | Want | Item |
|------|------|------|
| | | Food |
| | | Washer/Dryer |
| | | Magazine Subscription |
| | | New rims |
| | | Satellite Dish |
| | | Concert Tickets |
| | | Cell Phone |
| | | Designer Clothes |
| | | Child Care |
| | | Yoga pants |
| | | Convenience Foods |
| | | Gas/Electricity/Water |
| | | Eating Out |
| | | College/School Expenses |
| | | Car Insurance |
| | | Church Offering |
| | | Big Screen TV |
| | | House Payment/Rent |
| | | Clothes |

# Awareness

Have you ever reached the end of a month or a pay cycle, with your paycheck still five days away but with no money in your account? Maybe you tried to use your ATM card to pay for something and had the uncomfortable experience of being told by the store clerk that your card was declined. You probably wondered where all the money had gone.

It is important that you know where your money is going—this allows you to begin to control your money, rather than being controlled by it. I recommend that you begin right away by tracking everything, yes *everything*, that you spend for a week and then for a month. This tracking of every penny spent will give you an overview of where the money is going in a particular month. It's a kind of pre-budget step that will allow a starting point from which to build a realistic budget, one that acknowledges what you spend.

# Financial Stress Caused by Overindulgence

The desire for instant gratification is so tempting for many people. In many situations this desire is so overwhelming that wants begin to feel like needs, and this is where many people run into trouble with money management. They spend far too much money on their wants, sometimes using money that should be spent on needs. The real problem is that giving in to the pull of instant gratification is that it creates a cycle of long-term financial and emotional stress. Overindulging in wants tends to create a financial shortfall.

## EXERCISE #2

Your needs and wants. For this exercise, you will determine what your needs are and what needs are most important.

1. What are your needs?

_____

_____

_____

_____

_____

_____

_____

_____

_____

_____

**2.** Which of the items from your needs list are the most important? These are the items that you would pay for or buy each month and are based on your values – what's important to you and your family!

_____

_____

_____

_____

_____

_____

_____

_____

_____

_____

**3.** What are your wants?

_____

_____

_____

_____

_____

_____

_____

_____

_____

_____

# How to Stop the Cycle: Create and Stick to a Budget

As you can see, giving in to the desire for instant gratification and spending money on things you don't truly need creates a cycle of long-term financial and emotional stress, one that's difficult to get out of. Better not to get in this situation to begin with. But how can you avoid it? And if you already have debt, how can you avoid acquiring anymore? By creating and sticking to a budget. This is a matter of planning and exercising self-control, saying, "NO!" to most wants.

A budget is a plan for how you intend to spend money each month. Again, you've determined what is ok to spend money on and how much you can afford to spend in any category when you are not in the emotionally charged situation of being tempted by the desire for instant gratification.

But here's the big thing: because you have a logical plan, it becomes easier to say, "no," to items and services that you don't need and cannot really afford. In essence, a budget helps you to just say no sometimes, as you control your money rather than being controlled by it.

A Young Money Plan budget just for you can be found and downloaded on **youngmoneyplan.com**. To get you started today, your first exercise is to create a budget.

## EXERCISE #1

Using the template below, create your monthly budget. Remember to include every expense; this includes all of your entertainment, food, housing, cars, gas, clothes, toys, etc. Don't leave anything out!

## MONTHLY EXPENSE TRACKER

| | Expenses | Week 1 | Week 2 | Week 3 | Week 4 |
|---|---|---|---|---|---|
| LIVING | Rent | | | | |
| | Utilities | | | | |
| | Cable | | | | |
| | Phone | | | | |
| | Internet | | | | |
| | Furnishings | | | | |
| | Misc. | | | | MONTHLY TOTAL |
| | TOTAL | | | | |

| Expenses | Week 1 | Week 2 | Week 3 | Week 4 |
|---|---|---|---|---|
| Car Payment | | | | |
| Insurance | | | | |
| Fuel | | | | |
| Parking | | | | |
| Repairs | | | | |
| Public Trans. | | | | |
| Misc. | | | | |
| **TOTAL** | | | | |
| Doctor | | | | |
| Dentist | | | | |
| Eyes | | | | |
| Insurance | | | | |
| Prescriptions | | | | |
| Misc. | | | | |
| **TOTAL** | | | | |

TRANSPORTATION

MEDICAL

MONTHLY TOTAL

MONTHLY TOTAL

| Expenses | Week 1 | Week 2 | Week 3 | Week 4 | |
|---|---|---|---|---|---|
| **PERSONAL** Entertainment | | | | | |
| Cell Phone | | | | | |
| Clothing | | | | | |
| Laundry | | | | | |
| Toiletries | | | | | |
| Misc. | | | | | |
| **TOTAL** | | | | | MONTHLY TOTAL |
| **FOOD** Groceries | | | | | |
| Meal Plan | | | | | |
| Dining Out | | | | | |
| Misc. | | | | | |
| **TOTAL** | | | | | MONTHLY TOTAL |
| **OTHER** Loans | | | | | |
| Credit Cards | | | | | |
| Savings | | | | | |
| Investments | | | | | |
| Misc. | | | | | MONTHLY TOTAL |
| **TOTAL** | | | | | |

## Action Steps

In addition to the exercises above, complete the following action steps in order to successfully complete Step Three.

- Start today by tracking your spending. Record everything you spend for a week, then a month. It's as easy as snapping a cellphone photo of every receipt you get, when you get it. This will give you a picture (literally) of where you are currently spending money. Or you can write down your daily spending in your notes area of your cell phone or in a small notebook you carry with you or in your car.
- Pay attention to food and entertainment expenses. These two categories of spending are the biggest budget busters for most young people.
- Identify the difference between needs and wants. Before making any purchase, ask yourself whether it is a need or a want. Remember, needs are things you have to have to survive (food, water, housing, transportation, clothing) and wants are things you'd really like to have, but can survive without (video games, eating out instead of cooking at home, entertainment, sporting gear).
- Using the forms I've provided, write out a potential budget to implement next month. Feel free to adapt the forms to suit you and your situation.

# CHAPTER 4: STEP FOUR
# Get into the Game of Investing Automatically

This very exciting step instructs you how to begin creating wealth through the stock market with little investment required. I help you understand mutual funds, ETF's and the stock market as a whole better so you can take advantage of the power of automatic investing and the power of compound interest. Truly amazing.

Hold on to your hats as this step can make a tremendous difference in your life. Understanding investing can make a big impact on the other four steps in the Young Money 5 Step Plan. After automatically setting aside a sufficient amount in a savings account, or your "life happens" account, it is important that you start investing. Simply put, investing is a way to make your money multiply, even exponentially, over time. Some people feel intimidated by the idea of investing, but this is really only because they don't have the information to allow them to make informed choices. Investing is where the real fun happens, and you can enjoy the experience of watching your money grow. In fact, this step is my favorite step of the Young Money Plan because it can have a dramatic impact on how you begin to dream. Not only for your dreams but how you can positively affect the lives of other people along the way.

## The Time Value of Money

The value of money changes over time. Has your father or grandfather ever told you that the soda you purchase for $1.50 from a vending machine or fast food restaurant he purchased for $.15 when he was your age?

While the amount that a dollar can purchase has decreased over time, people are not necessarily experiencing a lower standard of living as a result. This is due to what we call inflation—as time goes on and due to a variety of factors, prices rise. In a healthy economy, this is offset by a rise in wages. In other words, although things tend to rise in cost over time, people also tend to make more over time, allowing them to be able to purchase about the same amount of goods that they were able to in the past, although at a higher cost.

But here's the take away for you: simply putting money away—hiding it under your mattress the way some people used to do—does nothing to increase the value of your money. If you simply squirrel money away for the future, you'll actually be able to buy *less* with that money than you would today.

## EXERCISE #1

Suppose you go in for an interview for a part-time job. The boss offers to pay you $50 a day for a 5-day, 10-week position OR you can earn only one cent on the first day but have your daily wage doubled every additional day you work. Which option would you take? Why?

_____

_____

_____

_____

_____

_____

_____

_____

_____

_____

_____

_____

_____

_____

_____

_____

# What Are Stocks?

Stocks are a portion of ownership in a company. Purchasing stock in a company, then, means buying a partial share of ownership and putting money towards a company's endeavors. Owning stock in a company also means sharing in a company's financial success. The financial success that a company enjoys is shared with stockholders or shareholders in payments called dividends. Often, investors choose to reinvest these dividends back into the company. Stocks are the basic building block of most investment portfolios.

# EXERCISE #2

Although everyone knows that the past history of a stock does not adequately predict the future of that same stock, knowing the history may help you *analyze* the possibility of a positive future return.

See if you know the direction of the following stocks from January 1 to October 31, 2013. Use arrows to illustrate your guess of the trend for each of the following stocks.

| Company | Stock Trader Symbol | Trend Direction |
|---|---|---|
| Apple Inc. | AAPL | |
| Intel Corp. | INTC | |
| General Electric Co. | GE | |
| Starbucks Corp. | SBUX | |
| Home Depot Inc. | HD | |
| Whole Foods Market | WFM | |
| New York Times Co. | NYT | |
| Toyota Motor Corp. | TM | |
| Costco Wholesale Corp. | COST | |

Among your group members, discuss which two companies you suspect had the strongest percentage of stock price growth for the period January 1 through October 31, 2013 and which two had the lowest (or negative) return. List the top two and lowest two below.

Top two:

#1 _____

#2 _____

Lowest two:

#1 _____

#2 _____

In addition, research the top two and the bottom two companies and determine what happenings in the companies led to the increase and decrease of the stock prices. Understanding the different factors that impact the stock price will make you a more informed investor. Report the findings below.

_____

_____

_____

_____

_____

_____

_____

_____

_____

_____

A great way to learn more about stocks and the stock market as a whole is to participate in a stock market simulation. I recommend **howthemarketworks.com**. You are given a virtual $25,000 - $1,000,000 to practice trading stocks, mutual funds and ETF's. **Youngmoneyplan.com** also offers a stock market simulation platform that is great for beginning investors.

# What Are Bonds?

Another type of investment is the bond. When you purchase a bond, you are basically loaning money to either a company or a government entity. When companies or municipalities, including state and national governments, issue bonds, they are basically raising funds by asking a number of people to make small loans towards a particular goal. These bonds are then paid back to the individual investors, with interest, at a stipulated period of time.

Bonds are generally lower risk than stocks, but this also means that the payoff tends to be lower as well. In this sense bonds are a "safer" investment than stocks. You know ahead of time what amount you will be getting in return and what the timeframe is for the return on your investment.

# What Are Mutual Funds?

Professional money managers oversee and operate mutual funds. An advantage of mutual funds over some other investment tools is that investors with relatively small amounts of capital can buy into a larger pool and thus be able to invest in diversified portfolios. The profit or loss any one investor experiences is proportional to the amount the investor has put into the fund.

Some mutual funds are guided by particular mission statements or interests. For example, some are dedicated strictly to investing in eco-friendly companies and programs. Some investors like this type of mutual fund because they are able to invest in a way that is guided by their values and conscience.

# What Are Exchange Traded Funds?

Exchange traded funds, or ETFs, are a relatively new investment product. They function like mutual funds in many ways: they are built of a variety of stocks and other investment tools, thus creating a diversified portfolio for a relatively small amount of money. Also, like mutual funds, ETFs are managed by professional investment managers.

The flexibility and especially the relatively low requirements for an initial investment make ETFs a particularly good choice for young investors. Even with just a small amount of initial capital, you can invest in an ETF, again making this a good place for young people to start.

# Automatic Investing

Quite simply, automatic investing means choosing to invest a specific, predetermined amount during a particular period, most likely each month or each pay period. In some ways this is similar to when I discussed automatically allocating part of each paycheck to a savings account. In a similar way, you can arrange through an investment firm to have a predetermined amount automatically deducted from your checking account each month and invested into any one of the investment tools discussed above. This is the key to creating wealth at a young age.

I highly recommend that not only do you invest a predetermined amount each month but that you simply let any interest or return on your investment sit, so that you can benefit from compound interest, as discussed above.

One really helpful thing about automatic investing is that it actually works to reduce your risk of losing money. Through a strategy called dollar-cost averaging, you are able to purchase more shares when the price is low and fewer when prices are high. Over time, this means that the price per share that you end up spending is lowered. Keep in mind that the stock market over the last 100 years has provided an average annual rate of return of nearly 11%. That type of return is better than any other asset class. And that is significant.

# How Investing Affects Your Spending and Overall Financial Outlook

Investing is an important piece of your long-term financial health. When you set up automatic investing each month and keep an eye towards your long-term financial goals, you can more easily say no to purchases that may be "wants" but not "needs."

Basically a commitment to investing means that each dollar you invest, rather than spend, will allow you to purchase more in the future. Because of the magic of compound interest, each dollar you save and invest will multiply over time, allowing you to actually purchase more.

## Action Steps

So what can you do now to begin investing? Here are steps you can take right away that will set you down a path of financial success:

- Decide how much you are going to invest automatically per month? Remember with many of the investment companies I recommend below there is not a minimum investment required. You can start with $25, $50 or $100.
- You can visit **youngmoneyplan.com** to implement this step with the investment companies we recommend.
- Set up automatic monthly withdrawal with the investment company you select so you can take advantage of the compound interest and dollar cost averaging.
- Once you've begun investing, leave that money alone. Do not withdraw any returns on your investment. Instead, take advantage of the time value of money
- Investing is for the long term (minimum 5 years).
- To further your investment gains open up a Roth IRA when you select your investment company. It will provide tax advantages over time.
- If you are employed and your company has a 401(k) plan contact your human resources department and ask how you can sign up. The company will likely match your investment by either 50 cents on each dollar or dollar per dollar which creates a superior investment return from the start.

## Recommended Investment Companies

In no particular order following are investment companies/brokerages I recommend to begin Step 4 of investing automatically per month to create wealth.

### ACORNS
acorns.com

Acorns is the first true micro investing company, allowing you to round up debit or credit card purchases to the nearest dollar and automatically invest the rest. How cool is that! You could easily begin investing $25 - $75 per month without much thought by simply using your debit card for purchases you already plan to make at fast food, gas stations, grocery store, iTunes, etc. The company was recently founded by father/son tandem Walter and Jeff Cruttenden. Walter knows a thing or two about investing as he helped E*Trade transition into online investing in the late 1990's. I relate to Jeff because he also began investing when he was very young and he has a similar passion for helping people reach financial goals and dreams through investing.

Acorns mission is to help young investors get started early and take advantage of the magic of compounding. It naturally aligns with Step 4 of the Young Money Plan as you can build wealth over time with minimal effort. The Acorns app and financial engine is built to help you invest commission-free into a diversified portfolio of index funds offered by the world's largest money managers: Vanguard, Blackrock, and PIMCO. You basically purchase fractional shares within the fund, automatically saving and investing small amounts of money frequently. In turn, the app automatically rebalances your portfolio positions for maximum performance. The Acorns app is fun to use and beautifully designed. Fees are very reasonable including a monthly service fee of $1.00. There is a 1% investment management fee per year but that drops to .25% once you reach $5,000 in your account.

Another way to describe Acorns is like the alarm app that helps you wake and the calendar app that helps you keep appointments, it works behind the scenes, saving and investing pennies at a time, so you don't have to. Small change may seem insignificant but history shows that even a dollar a day invested in a diversified portfolio of smaller companies over the last 50 years would be worth almost a million dollars today. I believe this micro investing app and platform will change the landscape in a big way for young and first time investors alike. From Acorns mighty oaks do grow!

## CAPITAL ONE SHAREBUILDER
sharebuilder.com

Capital One ShareBuilder enables you to invest in stocks, mutual funds and exchange traded funds (ETF's) with no account minimums. It is easy to open an account online, receive assistance by phone and they have great mobile apps to trade and monitor your investments. ShareBuilder has an "Automatic Investment Plan" which enables you to do Step 4 very easily. You choose the dollar amount you want to invest on a monthly or bi-weekly basis and every Tuesday your money will be withdrawn from your checking account and invested in stocks, an ETF or mutual fund. You can also trade individual stocks online with commissions as low as $6.95 per trade. ShareBuilder also has a Knowledge Center that is far from intimidating so you can understand tools, terms and investment types in no time.

## BETTERMENT
betterment.com

Betterment is an online and fully automated investing platform that enables you to invest in stock and bond ETF's designed to provide optimal and maximum investment returns. You can create specific goals with a time horizon and Betterment will help you reach those goals by allocating your dollars, re-investing dividends and minimizing taxes. Betterment gives you a wonderful user experience to engage with on your laptop, tablet or smartphone. Management fees are super cheap: charging only 35 cents for every $100 they manage and can go down to as low as 15 cents as your account balance grows over time. Betterment charges a monthly fee of $3.00 if you invest less than $100 per month which is not bad at all. Set your goal to $100 per month and the fee is gone.

## TD AMERITRADE
tdameritrade.com

I have always liked TD Ameritrade probably because my first brokerage account that was in my own name during college was Waterhouse Securities. Waterhouse was bought by TD Bank who then went on to buy Ameritrade. TD Ameritrade offers a very robust website to buy or trade individual stocks, mutual funds and ETF's. They have an exceptional learning and research center on their site. Unique to most big brokerages they do not have an account minimum to open up an account. Online stock trades are $9.99 and there are many commission and transaction free mutual funds and ETF's to choose from.

## T. ROWE PRICE
troweprice.com

One of the largest mutual fund companies in the world managing over $700 billion of individual and institutional money since 1937. T. Rowe Price offers over 75 mutual funds to invest in and has commission free representatives to help you choose which fund is right for you. Minimum investment for most of their funds is $1,000 but after that it goes down to $100 if you set up an automatic monthly investment plan. Hmm…sound familiar? Their management fees can range between .65 - 1 percent. As noted in the beginning of the book my first mutual fund at age 20 was the T. Rowe Price Science and Technology Fund.

# CHAPTER 5: STEP FIVE
# Pay Yourself Second

Conventional advice about money management says to pay yourself first, or to put part of your paycheck into savings or investments before doing anything else. However, giving is much more important than paying yourself first. I've coined the phrase "if you are not giving, you are not living." In this chapter I will help you identify where and how you can give now in order to make a short term and long term impact on others. There simply is no better feeling.

Earlier, in Step 2, I encouraged you to "pay" yourself first. And by this, I meant that before spending any of your income, you should automatically designate a portion of your paycheck to go into a savings, or a "life happens," account. The goal in paying yourself first is to begin to work towards larger financial goals. And certainly, automatically saving is an important step. It's not always easy, but it allows for financial freedom and allows you to work towards the dreams you identified in Step 1.

However, I want to revise this advice a bit: it is important that you actually pay yourself not first, but second. By this, I mean that it is necessary, before you think about how money can work for you that you should consider charitable giving of some sort. Although financial success can be tremendously helpful in this life, money and the acquisition of material goods should never be anyone's primary goal in life. Money on its own cannot give you a sense of purpose, and living a purposeful life is ultimately where you can find peace and success. To accomplish this, then, you must develop a mindset that encourages you to use your money towards a greater good.

# Money Cannot Create Purpose or Peace in Our Lives

On its own, money does not create the kind of peace, passion, and purpose that humans need in order to be fulfilled. That's right—money cannot give us the sense of purpose that humans need in order to be fulfilled. Instead, humans need to contribute to some cause outside themselves, some greater good in order to be fulfilled and truly happy. One way to begin to do this is through charitable giving.

I have been urging you to manage your money in such a way as to put it to work for you. And certainly I believe this is important. However, I don't want you to fall into the trap of believing that making money will, on its own, make you or anyone else happy. True happiness and peace come from living a life that is filled with purpose. This can be achieved only when we look beyond ourselves and commit to making the world around us a better place. Certainly we can use money to do that. In this way, money actually can buy some measure of happiness. Remember, if you are not giving, you are not living.

## EXERCISE #1

For this activity, you will research a few non-profit organizations to determine which one you would consider giving money to. Below is a list of charities. For each charity, write a few things that you learned about each.

### St. Jude Children's Research Hospital

_____

_____

_____

_____

### Save the Children

_____

_____

_____

_____

Juvenile Diabetes Research Foundation

_____

_____

_____

_____

Elizabeth Glazer Pediatric AIDS Foundation

_____

_____

_____

_____

The World Wildlife Fund

_____

_____

_____

_____

Operation Smile

_____

_____

_____

_____

UNICEF

_____

_____

_____

_____

**Marine Toys for Tots Foundation**

_____
_____
_____
_____

**Make-a-Wish Foundation**

_____
_____
_____
_____

**Hole in the Wall Camps**

_____
_____
_____
_____

**The Humane Society**

_____
_____
_____
_____

## Donation Based Crowdfunding

There is has been a growth in charitable giving through crowdfunding. In addition to well known charities, your local church, local and international ministries you may find a cause to support monthly by going to crowdfunding sites like: GoFundMe.com, Crowdrise.com, PureCharity.com and Indiegogo.com.

## Determining How Often & How Much to Give

Many organizations and businesses elect to donate monthly, with a bonus donation at Christmas or at the end of each financial quarter. Others choose to make a lump sum donation at the beginning or end of each year. Some organizations have 'wish lists' of machinery, appliances, supplies and items they need year round. Ask if a charity you're considering has such a list. Donate when and, as you're able to meet specific needs.

How you give depends on your situation. If you do decide to give once or twice a year, set aside the funds each week or month to ensure the money is there when it comes time to write the check.

There is no right or wrong amount to give. Organizations appreciate every donation they get. Don't worry about competing with other businesses or individuals over donation amounts either. It's not a competition. Give as you feel you can give. If money isn't an option, consider giving 'in-kind' donations of time, resources, materials or equipment loans.

## Action Steps

- Choose a charity or cause that has meaning to you
- Determine how much money, based on the budget you completed, that you could give each month to the charity
- Remember that volunteering your time is also important.

Congrats! You have mastered the 5 steps for building your financial future. In the following sections, you will be introduced to additional financial information.

# CHAPTER 6
# Other Personal Finance Stuff (Credit, Debt, & Taxes)

Many people are unaware of the tremendous burden that debt can create in their lives. Young people especially don't have a clear understanding of the pitfalls of credit cards and credit card debt. Good financial health includes a clear understanding of debt, credit, credit scores and taxes.

Another major area in which young adults lack knowledge and experience is purchasing a vehicle, paying for housing, and understanding the value of insurance. We all need a place to live and insurance. Most Americans need a car. Again, good financial health requires a clear understanding of managing money in these areas.

Good financial health means a healthy or good credit score, no more than a 30 percent utilization of your total allotted credit, a savings account with at least three months of living expenses (rent, utilities, etc.) socked away for emergencies, and investments in stocks, bonds and other resources. If you're financially healthy you have money set aside for emergencies as well as bills. If you need to buy a car, you have the down payment. If you want to take a vacation, fly to a job interview, volunteer to help build a school in Africa, you have the money. While money can't buy happiness, it can buy choices. And it's choices that make us happy, fulfilled and productive.

In this section, we will focus on credit cards and your credit score.

## Credit Cards

In today's financial world, credit cards are a common part of a consumer's financial plan. Credit cards are not always a bad idea, but it is important to not get carried away in using them! Credit cards are not for everyone! You need to understand when to use them and when to just say no.

Credit cards are a form of financing. Financial institutions provide consumers with credit cards that contain a certain credit line or balance depending on your credit score, income, credit history, and other factors. The balance or limit you are given on the card is the amount of credit you have to spend. When you charge something to the card, you are also charged a certain interest rate for the amount you have used if you do not pay your balance in full each month. One important thing to remember is only paying the minimum payment on your card will mean a longer time period of repayment and the more interest you will end up paying in the end!

You can talk to three different people and each person likely has a different view of credit cards. One of the reasons why credit cards are viewed as negative is the amount of debt consumers have racked up in credit card debt. There are consumers that tend to spend outside their means because the credit cards provide money that they normally would not have. This means they are borrowing money that they don't have! When a certain amount of credit card debt is accrued, it can be difficult to pay it off and get out of debt. This is the bad and evil that many people feel about credit cards.

If used correctly, credit cards can be a positive financial tool. Credit cards do protect you from fraud. If someone steals your card, the credit card company will reimburse you for the fraudulent purchases. If you carried cash, no one would reimburse you if your money was stolen. Also, credit cards are not tied to your checking account. This means if someone accesses your credit card, they only have access to the amount of money on your card and not the entire balance of your checking account. Finally, credit card companies offer rewards and free items for using their cards. If used and managed correctly, credit cards can be another tool to use to manage your money and your finances.

Your credit utilization rate comprises 30 percent of your total credit score. A credit utilization rate is the ratio of your credit card balances to your credit card limits as listed on your credit report. For instance, if you have a credit card limit of $1,000 and your credit card balance (what you owe) is $300, then your credit utilization is 30 percent, right where it should be. Even if you're paying off your bills in full every month, using more than the 30 percent of credit you're allotted can lower your score. The lower your credit utilization the better, because it shows you're only using a small amount of the credit that you've been given. To find out what your current credit utilization is, find your total credit limit on all your accounts. Divide your credit card balances (what you owe), by your credit limit then multiply by 100.

## EXERCISE #1

For Exercise #1, you will have the opportunity to research a credit card company and one of the credit cards that they offer. Based on your research, you will answer the following questions:

- Choose a credit card company. Some examples are Citi Cards, Discover, Capital One, Bank of America, Wells Fargo, etc.
- After you have chosen the credit card company, select one of the cards they offer. Based on that card, answer the following questions.
  1. What is the interest rate for the card?
  2. Are there any fees involved?
     - Annual fee
     - Transaction fee

- Late fee
- Other fees
3. What other information did you find important?

Part of being financially sound is knowing the right questions to ask. The more informed you are, the better decisions you can make.

# Credit Score

Do you know your number? No, not your weight, age, telephone number; I mean your credit score. These three little numbers say a lot about your current and financial future. There is no greater time than now to understand your credit score and what it means for you.

Your credit score, or your FICO score as it is commonly called, provides a score of your credit worthiness. Any time you apply for a loan, fill out a job application, try to rent an apartment, etc. your credit report will be obtained to see if you are financially sound. Your credit score is the number of your financial life and will impact many areas. Your number says whether you are a good or bad credit risk.

# Determining the Credit Score

Have you ever wondered how your credit score is actually determined? You may not think it is important to know how credit scores are determined, but it actually is. This is because you can control some of the factors that make-up your credit score. Your credit score is based on the information found on your credit report and is evaluated against the millions of other people's credit score. Below is a graphic with the five general categories that determine your credit score.

Credit scores range from 850 to 579. A score of 850 would be the best and

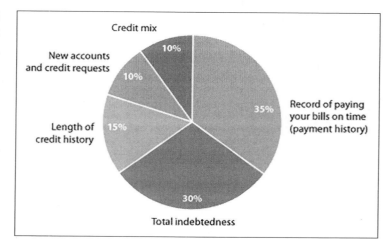

579 would the lowest a credit score could be. The median FICO score today is 720 out of a possible 850. Consumers that have a 600 or less are considered the riskiest customers. The score matters for many reasons, but one of the reasons is the interest rate that you will receive for large purchases such as an auto, home or business loan. higher credit score usually results in lower interest rates on those same large purchases. So, your credit score impacts how much you pay!

**730+**
excellent credit

**700-729**
good/above average

**670-699**
good credit

**585-669**
fair credit

**584 or below**
poor credit

# Grow Your Credit Score!

So, now that you understand what determines your credit score, it is important to consider the ways that you can improve your score or make sure your score does not fall lower.

The first way is your payment history. It is important to pay your bills on-time. If you are currently late on any payments, get current as soon as you can. The longer a payment is late, the more detrimental this will be to your credit score. Remember that if you have a history of late payments, closing or paying off the loan or credit card will not make the negative history go away.

The second way to improve your credit score is to keep your balances low. If you have a credit card, try to keep that balance at 30 percent or less of your available balance. Maxed out credit cards are almost as negative as late payments. In addition, instead of doing balance transfers or moving around the debt from one place to the next, try to pay it off. Finally, do not close unused credit cards. This will lower your score.

The third way to improve your credit score is with new credit. If you have a history of credit problems, re-establishing your credit history is important. If you can find a lender to give you a short-term loan and a low balance loan, this is a good start. Just remember to make the payments timely or your credit score will not increase, but be hurt worse. Also, don't open too much credit at once.

Finally, here are few key tips to remember about your credit score:

- Unpaid medical bills do impact your credit score.
- Large amounts of credit can hurt your score.
- Credit scores decrease with too many inquiries, so don't sign-up for retailer's credit card just to receive the discount!

The best paying jobs are often linked to financial responsibility—banks, stores, accounting, customer service, management and more. Poor credit scores can knock you out of the running for good-paying jobs in many industries, including emergency services, law enforcement, medical and financial fields.

You may be able to afford a nice apartment, but a poor credit score is one of the primary reasons most young (and older) people are denied on housing applications. Even if you can show proof of income, with a poor credit score you'll most likely have to provide a large deposit and/or have a cosigner.

## EXERCISE #2
### Determining the Credit Score

For this activity, please visit the following website: **https://www.annualcreditreport.com/index.action**. This site allows you to obtain a copy of your credit report from three main reporting agencies. This is a free service and does not hurt your credit score. For this activity, review at least one of the three reports. If you choose to, you may purchase your credit score from the reporting agency after viewing the report.

## EXERCISE #3
### Assessment of Credit Report

After reviewing your credit report, did you have anything on your credit report that you were not aware of?

_____

_____

_____

_____

## EXERCISE #4
### Improving your Credit Score

After reading through the material, what areas do you need to improve upon to increase your credit score? Create a plan of action below for achieving success in these areas.

_____

_____

_____

_____

_____

# Taxes

Taxes are an everyday fact of life. You pay taxes when receive a paycheck or make a purchase. Most people pay taxes in four major categories: taxes on purchases, taxes on property, taxes on wealth and taxes on earnings.

Taxes on purchases is called a **sales tax**. So if you go to the mall and buy a new pair of jeans, a pair of shoes or another piece of clothing you will be paying sales tax on those items. However, many states exempt food and drugs from sales tax to reduce the financial burden on low income households. An **excise tax** is imposed by the federal and state governments on specific goods and services such as gasoline, cigarettes, alcohol and air travel.

A second type of tax is **property tax**. Real estate property tax is a major source of revenue for local governments and is based on the value of land, commercial buildings and homes.

Taxes on wealth include an **estate tax** which is imposed on the value of a person's property at the time of death. This federal tax is typically based on the fair market value of the deceased person's investments, property and bank accounts. Money and property passed on to heirs may be subject to an **inheritance tax**. This tax is paid for the right to acquire the inherited property.

The final tax category is taxes on earnings. The two main taxes on wages and salaries are **Social Security and income taxes**. The Federal Insurance Contributions Act (FICA) created the Social Security tax to fund old-age, survivors and disability insurance portion of the Social Security system and the hospital insurance portion otherwise known as Medicare.

Most workers are subject to federal, state and even local income tax from their earnings. Only seven states do not have an income tax. Your employer will typically withhold income tax payments from your paycheck or if you own your own business you will make estimated tax payments. Both types of payments are estimates and you may owe more tax or receive a tax refund after the tax year has ended. The more you know about taxes the more it will help you with your personal financial plan.

# CHAPTER 7

# More Personal Finance Stuff (Buying a Car, Insurance and Housing)

Major purchases should fit in your current budget and also fit in with your long-term goals. Before you decide to make a purchase, you should always review your personal budget to make sure you that you have the discretionary income to take on a new payment or the cash to buy the item outright. You should be able to live within your income even after you make the purchase. No purchase is ever worth putting yourself in financial difficulty. Remember to consider any unexpected changes that you might experience, such as a job change or loss or a change in your current family situation. These changes might take more of your discretionary income, so being prepared can help you avoid any financial difficulties. You should always have a savings cushion available to cover these unexpected changes. Buying a car or a house can be an exciting time, but it is still important to think logically and do your homework.

## Buying a Car

If you have ever gone through the car buying process, you know that it is not as easy as just pulling up to the auto dealer and making the purchase. If you want to find the best deal for your money, you need to put some work in! Buying a car is something that we will all likely do at some point in time. There are many options available when it comes to selecting and buying a car.

The first major decision is to buy new or used. There are certainly pros and cons to both. When you buy a new car, you will likely have a warranty for about five years of 100,000 miles, whichever one comes first. When you buy used, there would be no warranty and you buy "as is." This can be risky.

On the other side, when you buy a new car, most cars will depreciate 10 – 15% percent once you drive it off the lot! This means that you would avoid the huge depreciation and mark-up of the vehicle's price if you buy used. You can see that you have key decisions and trade-offs to make here.

## EXERCISE #1

For this exercise, you will consider all of the pros and cons of buying a new car versus buying a used car. Please use the spaces below to make the comparisons. A few suggestions are provided to get you started, but please add in your own criteria as well.

| Criteria | New Car | Used Car |
|---|---|---|
| Price | | |
| Reliability/Warranty | | |
| Gas | | |
| Insurance | | |
| Look/Appeal | | |
| Down payment | | |
| Interest rate | | |
| Resale value | | |
| | | |
| | | |
| | | |
| | | |

Another key decision you will need to make when buying a vehicle is where to purchase the vehicle. You have the option of going to a traditional dealership or buying the vehicle from a private individual. There are websites, such as Craigslist, cars.com, carsforsale.com, and more that bring people together for the purpose of selling their vehicles. Let's consider your options in Exercise #2.

## EXERCISE #2

For this Exercise, consider the type of vehicle you would like. Complete the following information to narrow down your search criteria:

- Year _____
- Make _____
- Model _____
- Mileage _____
- Required Features _____
- Location _____
- Price _____

Now that you have your vehicle search criteria narrowed down, visit websites of traditional car dealerships and also secondary sites, such as the peer-to-peer sites mentioned above. If you are in college, many manufactures like Toyota, Southeast Toyota, Honda, General Motors, Ford and Hyundai offer additional incentives within their College Graduate Program. Some car companies offer $400 - $1,000 off a new vehicle upon showing proof you are a student or have recently graduated. Using the criteria you listed above, research the prices of the similar vehicles. Record your findings below:

_____
_____
_____
_____
_____
_____
_____

You should now be prepared to make an informed decision about how, where, and what type of vehicle to purchase. Remember; make sure your purchase fits with your financial status now and in the future.

# Choosing Your Home

In Chapter 7, we discussed the different specifications about purchasing a home. Home ownership is very important and will likely be the biggest investment that you will ever make. Likely, if you are in college, about to graduate, or have graduated, your biggest housing decision will be whether to rent or buy. There are certainly pros and cons to both decisions.

## EXERCISE #3

Should you rent or buy? This is a decision that you will face at some point in your life and the decision is not a simple one to make. The answer depends on your readiness, your finances, and where you want to be in the future. Most of you know about the housing crisis in our country that started in 2006-2007. Simply stated many people were buying homes that they simply could not afford and some people only put 5% or less down on the home. Prices of homes plunged across the nation which left millions of homeowners (some still today) with no equity in their home. If you are considering buying a home my recommendation is to save enough over several years so you can put down at least 25% of the home's purchase price. This will give you adequate equity to start your journey to not only paying off your home mortgage over time but having some financial peace while enjoying your home at the same time.

For this exercise, you will complete the rent vs buying tool from the following website:

**http://www.realtor.com/home-finance/tools/rent-or-buy-calculator/**

After completing the required information (location, home amount you want, and rent amount you want), you will be presented with a summary of the net costs that will help you compare the amount of money you would spend over time. Record your findings below and state which option is the best for you based on the findings.

# Insurance

Insurance can be purchased for your property and your home, your health, and other major assets. In each case, you weigh the cost of the consequence of a risk that may never actually happen against the cost of insuring against it. Deciding what and how to insure is really a process of deciding what the costs of loss would be and how willing you are to pay to get rid of those risks.

## EXERCISE #4

At this stage of your life, you likely are focused mostly on car insurance and renter's insurance or homeowner's insurance. One important consideration to make about insurance is the amount that you pay. There are many insurance companies to choose from, so it is important to comparison shop in order to find the best deal. For this activity, you will comparison shop for one type of insurance that you currently have. Before you can comparison shop, make sure you compare apples to apples by deciding on the different coverages you want. Consider the following:

- Deductible Amounts
- Full coverage vs liability ( for vehicle)
- Payments (yearly, semi-annual, or monthly)
- Discounts for multi-products with same company

Now, that you have your criteria, you can begin your research. Record your findings in the table below:

| Insurance Company | Price | Deductibles | Coverage Type | Other Information |
|---|---|---|---|---|
| | | | | |
| | | | | |
| | | | | |
| | | | | |
| | | | | |

Remember, these are major purchases and decisions that you need to consider carefully. Buying a home, purchasing a car, and having the right protection of you and your assets are key areas to ensure your financial health in the future.

# CHAPTER 8: ENTREPRENEUR MINDSET
# A Must Have to Get Ahead with Money

Do you have dreams of starting your own business one day? Well, if you said, yes, you would not be alone. According to the Kaufman Foundation, over 51 percent of the millennial generation plan to start their own business versus work for an employer, and for those that are working for someone else, 71 percent of millennial employees have a dream of owning their own business. With today's technology, this generation is realizing that all you need is a computer and seed money to get started. Let's consider the key factors you need to consider before deciding to become an entrepreneur.

## EXERCISE #1

When you decide to make good financial decisions now, this will benefit you should you become a business owner. Finance issues play a major role in the failure of many small businesses. Learning the key concepts of your finances today will prepare you to make better financial decisions in the future. To determine your financial habits, complete the short self-assessment on the next page:

To start your self-assessment, and motivate yourself to do better, complete the following quiz. Mark A for Always, S for Sometimes and N for Never.

As a rule, do you:

|  |  | A | S | N |
|---|---|---|---|---|
| 1. | Refrain from over drafting your account | ☐ | ☐ | ☐ |
| 2. | Maintain more than $25 in your account | ☐ | ☐ | ☐ |
| 3. | Keep an "in case of emergency" fund | ☐ | ☐ | ☐ |
| 4. | Plan ahead for large expenses such as buying a car or moving into an apartment | ☐ | ☐ | ☐ |
| 5. | Set goals and keep a budget for your net income | ☐ | ☐ | ☐ |
| 6. | Comparison shop for the purchase of most items | ☐ | ☐ | ☐ |
| 7. | Only pay for things you have the money in the bank to cover | ☐ | ☐ | ☐ |
| 8. | Balance your checkbook or frequently utilize online banking | ☐ | ☐ | ☐ |
| 9. | Keep yourself financially updated by reading personal financial articles and magazines | ☐ | ☐ | ☐ |

If the majority of resulting checked boxes is:

**A – Always**       **RELAX** – You possess very good personal financial habits and behavior. Congratulations!

**S – Sometimes**    **BE CAUTIOUS** – You may need to change some personal financial habits and behaviors. Be aware and take steps to learn more about managing your finances.

**N – Never**        **DANGER** – You may be in danger of losing control of your personal financial situation. Act now to take control of your finances by checking out resources available from the Student Financial Management Center.

*Source: Money Management International's Understanding Money and Credit Reference Guide*

**After completing the assessment, how do you feel about your financial habits? What would you like to change?**

_____

_____

_____

_____

_____

_____

_____

**Now that you know what you would like to change, describe below your goals and action plan for making these financial changes.**

_____

_____

_____

_____

_____

_____

_____

_____

**Based on the results of the assessment, do you believe you have the financial habits to be a successful entrepreneur? Explain.**

_____

_____

_____

_____

_____

_____

_____

Another key component of being an entrepreneur is to craft the idea you have for a business venture. There are many entrepreneurs who have turned their hobbies into major businesses.

# EXERCISE #2

Let's discuss your hobbies and potential income streams. In the space below, think of your top three hobbies. After doing so, brainstorm ways that you could turn your hobby into a business. Finally, describe the pros and cons of this opportunity.

_____

_____

_____

_____

_____

_____

_____

_____

_____

_____

_____

_____

_____

_____

_____

_____

_____

_____

_____

_____

_____

_____

# CHAPTER 9
# The Young Money Plan Movement and 5 Point Checklist

Congratulations! You have made it to the end of this guidebook. By doing so you have made it clear that you don't want the status quo with your financial future. So let's get rolling. The following exercises will take you through the 5 Step Plan action steps so you can begin your own personal Young Money Plan. These exercises are similar to the exercise steps you completed in Chapters 1-5. You can use them as a reference.

## EXERCISE #1
### Step One: Make A Decision to Dream.

Fill out your personal "Dream Sheet" by visiting **youngmoneyplan.com** and print it out. Or you can get a sheet of paper or a dream notebook. Write down your short term, mid-range, and long term dreams and goals. Be specific. "I want to save a lot of money this year" or "I want to have a really nice car" is too general. It is very important to make your goals personal and not what the world tells you are important or valuable. Money is personal and has different meanings for different people. Have fun going through this process. Dreaming and goal setting is the motivation to build financial confidence that can lead to a much fuller and richer life!

## EXERCISE #2
### Step Two: Set Up Your Automatic Savings Plan.

This is super easy and you will be so glad you did it.

- If you don't have a checking or savings account, open one up today by visiting a bank or credit union. Or through an online bank. There should be no cost to you.

- Have a predetermined dollar amount transferred from your checking to your savings account on a monthly basis AUTOMATICALLY. You can set it up on your bank or credit union's website or tell them at the branch. You can choose any day of the month for the automatic transfer to occur like the 15th or 25th of each month.
- It does not matter the dollar amount you start with. By starting with only $10, you are creating a savings habit. That number will increase over time because you realize how your savings account is helping you cover unexpected expenses that life brings to all of us.
- Eventually create multiple savings accounts so you have the money on hand when you need it for things you need and want over time. A savings account for clothes, entertainment, future car, vacation, etc... You can begin saving a predetermined amount into each savings category automatically.
- Visit **youngmoneyplan.com** to open up a bank account with one of our preferred banking partner(s).

## EXERCISE #3

### Step Three: Create Your Personal Spending Plan

- Start today by tracking your spending. Record everything you spend for a week, then a month. It's as easy as snapping a cellphone photo of every receipt you get, when you get it. This will give you a picture (literally) of where you are currently spending money. Or you can write down your daily spending in your notes area of your cell phone. Or in a small notebook you carry with you.
- Identify the difference between needs and wants. Before making any purchase, ask yourself whether it is a need or a want. Remember, needs are things you have to have to survive ( food, water, housing, transportation, clothing) and wants are things you'd really like to have, but can survive without (video games, eating out instead of cooking at home, entertainment, second pair of running shoes, etc.).
- Know your average monthly income so you can compare your fixed and variable expenses. Making sure you have more income than expenses.
- Create your own personal budget by visiting **youngmoneyplan.com**.

## EXERCISE #4

### Step Four: Start Your Automatic Investment Account

- I listed several companies in Chapter 4 that I recommend to begin an investment account. Most of them have no minimum investment requirement.
- Get comfortable with some or all of them by visiting their website that I listed. Then if you want to get even more comfortable you can call their toll free telephone number listed on their website. They can give you guidance on which mutual fund or ETF to begin with. I recommend growth stock mutual funds or S&P 500 ETF.
- After you are comfortable and have completed Steps 1, 2 and 3 then open up an investment account.
- Elect to have an automatic investment plan established from the beginning by having $25, $50 or $100 AUTOMATICALLY transferred from your checking to your investment account every month. Just like Step 2 you can choose the 15th or 25th of each month.

- You have gone from a spectator to a participant in the game of investing. And you are taking advantage of "Dollar Cost Averaging" by investing every month.
- Visit **youngmoneyplan.com** to see a list of our preferred investment companies.

## EXERCISE #5

### Step Five: Pay Yourself Second by Giving First

- Consider charities and causes that you can not only provide financial support to, but also your personal time. Consider charities and causes you identified in Chapter 5.

# Summary

When it comes to financial independence, knowledge is key! It is important to remember to protect your family and your money. Being smart by understanding different ways to make money, how to save money, and the key factors that impact your credit will help you to obtain financial freedom. It is important to remember that even if you don't have a lot of money, you can still save and protect your credit.

**So, remember the 5 Step Money Plan:**

**Step One –Dream.** Make A Decision To Dream.

**Step Two – Save.** Set up an Automatic Savings Plan.

**Step Three – Spend.** Create a Realistic Spending Plan. Establish a monthly budget that highlights income, fixed and variable expenses and tracks how you are doing.

**Step Four – Invest.** Get Into the Game of Investing.

**Step Five – Give.** Giving back is an important aspect of everyone's life and the younger you start, the more it will become a part of your routine.

You can also visit **Youngmoneyplan.com** for valuable tools, coaching, and more guidance on implementing the Young Money Plan for yourself.

In the following pages, you will have the opportunity to journal about your experiences and also provide updates on your goals.

# GOAL UPDATES #1

| Short-Term Goals | Progress Update |
| --- | --- |
| Goal #1 | |
| Goal #2 | |
| Goal #3 | |
| Goal #4 | |
| Goal #5 | |

| Mid-Range Goals | Progress Update |
| --- | --- |
| Goal #1 | |

| Mid-Range Goals | Progress Update |
|---|---|
| Goal #2 | |
| Goal #3 | |

| Long-Term Goals | Progress Update |
|---|---|
| Goal #1 | |
| Goal #2 | |
| Goal #3 | |
| Goal #4 | |
| Goal #5 | |

# GOAL UPDATES #2

| Short-Term Goals | Progress Update |
|---|---|
| Goal #1 | |
| Goal #2 | |
| Goal #3 | |
| Goal #4 | |
| Goal #5 | |

| Mid-Range Goals | Progress Update |
|---|---|
| Goal #1 | |

| Mid-Range Goals | Progress Update |
|---|---|
| Goal #2 | |
| Goal #3 | |

| Long-Term Goals | Progress Update |
|---|---|
| Goal #1 | |
| Goal #2 | |
| Goal #3 | |
| Goal #4 | |
| Goal #5 | |

# GOAL UPDATES #3

| Short-Term Goals | Progress Update |
| --- | --- |
| Goal #1 | |
| Goal #2 | |
| Goal #3 | |
| Goal #4 | |
| Goal #5 | |

| Mid-Range Goals | Progress Update |
| --- | --- |
| Goal #1 | |

| Mid-Range Goals | Progress Update |
|---|---|
| Goal #2 | |
| Goal #3 | |

| Long-Term Goals | Progress Update |
|---|---|
| Goal #1 | |
| Goal #2 | |
| Goal #3 | |
| Goal #4 | |
| Goal #5 | |

# GOAL UPDATES #4

| Short-Term Goals | Progress Update |
|---|---|
| Goal #1 | |
| Goal #2 | |
| Goal #3 | |
| Goal #4 | |
| Goal #5 | |

| Mid-Range Goals | Progress Update |
|---|---|
| Goal #1 | |

| Mid-Range Goals | Progress Update |
|---|---|
| Goal #2 | |
| Goal #3 | |

| Long-Term Goals | Progress Update |
|---|---|
| Goal #1 | |
| Goal #2 | |
| Goal #3 | |
| Goal #4 | |
| Goal #5 | |

# GOAL UPDATES #5

| Short-Term Goals | Progress Update |
|---|---|
| Goal #1 | |
| Goal #2 | |
| Goal #3 | |
| Goal #4 | |
| Goal #5 | |

| Mid-Range Goals | Progress Update |
|---|---|
| Goal #1 | |

| Mid-Range Goals | Progress Update |
|---|---|
| Goal #2 | |
| Goal #3 | |

| Long-Term Goals | Progress Update |
|---|---|
| Goal #1 | |
| Goal #2 | |
| Goal #3 | |
| Goal #4 | |
| Goal #5 | |

# MENTOR NOTES #1

In this section, your mentor will provide observations of how you are doing going through the five steps.

_____

_____

_____

_____

_____

_____

_____

_____

_____

_____

_____

_____

_____

_____

_____

_____

_____

_____

_____

_____

_____

_____

_____

_____

_____

_____

_____

# MENTOR NOTES #2

In this section, your mentor will provide observations of how you are doing going through the five steps.

_____

_____

_____

_____

_____

_____

_____

_____

_____

_____

_____

_____

_____

_____

_____

_____

_____

_____

_____

_____

_____

_____

_____

_____

_____

_____

_____

_____

_____

_____

_____

# MENTOR NOTES #3

In this section, your mentor will provide observations of how you are doing going through the five steps.

# MENTOR NOTES #4

In this section, your mentor will provide observations of how you are doing going through the five steps.

_____
_____
_____
_____
_____
_____
_____
_____
_____
_____
_____
_____
_____
_____
_____
_____
_____
_____
_____
_____
_____
_____
_____
_____

# MENTOR NOTES #5

In this section, your mentor will provide observations of how you are doing going through the five steps.

_____

_____

_____

_____

_____

_____

_____

_____

_____

_____

_____

_____

_____

_____

_____

_____

_____

_____

_____

_____

_____

_____

_____

_____

_____

_____

_____

_____

# YOUR JOURNAL NOTES #1

In this section, journal about your journey as you worked through the five steps.

_____

_____

_____

_____

_____

_____

_____

_____

_____

_____

_____

_____

_____

_____

_____

_____

_____

_____

_____

_____

_____

_____

_____

_____

_____

_____

# YOUR JOURNAL NOTES #2

In this section, journal about your journey as you worked through the five steps.

_____

_____

_____

_____

_____

_____

_____

_____

_____

_____

_____

_____

_____

_____

_____

_____

_____

_____

_____

_____

_____

_____

_____

_____

_____

_____

_____

_____

# YOUR JOURNAL NOTES #3

In this section, journal about your journey as you worked through the five steps.

# YOUR JOURNAL NOTES #4

In this section, journal about your journey as you worked through the five steps.

_____

_____

_____

_____

_____

_____

_____

_____

_____

_____

_____

_____

_____

_____

_____

_____

_____

_____

_____

_____

_____

_____

_____

_____

_____

_____

_____

_____

_____

_____

_____

# YOUR JOURNAL NOTES #5

In this section, journal about your journey as you worked through the five steps.

_____

_____

_____

_____

_____

_____

_____

_____

_____

_____

_____

_____

_____

_____

_____

_____

_____

_____

_____

_____

_____

_____

_____

_____

_____

_____

_____

_____

_____